BOOKS TOO GOOD TO MISS

Creative Thinking with Books

Written and Illustrated by
Faye Day   Annette Geistfeld

120 CREATIVE CORNER

4175 Lovell Road

Circle Pines, MN 55014

120 CREATIVE CORNER
4175 Lovell Road
Circle Pines, MN 55014

Library of Congress Cataloging in Publication Data

Day, Faye
    Books Too Good To Miss.

    1. Creative Thinking.   2. Children's Literature

I. Geistfeld, Annette L., joint author.
II. Title.

ISBN 0 912773-04-9

TABLE OF CONTENTS

WHAT THIS BOOK IS ABOUT

Books Too Good to Miss is designed for classroom teachers and students, grades one through six. Its intention is to encourage student involvement with literature.

In the activities that follow, we've used theory-based thinking processes and research as vehicles through which to view children's books. These activities are designed to attract children to literature and in so doing, provide pleasure and stretch the imagination.

POSSIBLE USES FOR THIS BOOK

Use this book for:

-- building appreciation for good literature

-- integrating literature into the curriculum

-- enrichment for Reading classes

-- learning centers about books

-- topic studies

    e.g. Nutrition
            Bread and Jam For Frances
    e.g. Death and Dying
            The Tenth Good Thing About Barney

-- extra credit

-- parental use at home

-- reinforcement in thinking and research strategies

DEFINITION OF TERMS

PRODUCTIVE THINKING STRATEGIES:

FLUENCY
  Think of many responses; emphasis is on the quantity
  of ideas and not the quality.

FLEXIBILITY
  Think in a variety of categories by shifting thinking from one way into different ways of thinking.

ORIGINALITY
  Think of unusual or uncommon ideas that are clever,
  unique, and relevant but not obvious.

ELABORATION
  Add details to an idea to make it more interesting
  and complete.

EVALUATION
  Weigh ideas in terms of the desirability and
  undesirability of each.

PLANNING:

  The following steps need to be taken:
  1. Identify the task to be accomplished.
  2. List the materials needed.
  3. List in order the steps necessary to carry out
      the task.
  4. List problems which may be encountered in
      carrying out the plan.

FORECASTING:

  Consider many possible causes and effects of a
  situation, examine the quality of the responses,
  choose the strongest cause and effect and give reasons
  for each choice.

COMMUNICATION STRATEGIES:

DESCRIPTION WITHIN CATEGORIES
Describe an object or situation from several points
of view i.e. how it looks, feels, smells, sounds,
and uses of the object.

COMPARISONS AND RELATIONSHIPS
Use words and ideas to make comparisons between
things, to show relationships or associations.

COMPOSITION
Organize words and ideas into meaningful patterns
and products.

QUESTIONING
Develop higher level questioning skills which go
beyond the factual and comprehension level questions.

MORE INFORMATION ABOUT THESE BOOKS

Albert's Toothache
by Barbara Williams
E.P. Dutton, New York
ISBN 0-525-25368-8

Bread and Jam For Frances
by Russell Hoban
Scholastic Book Services
ISBN 0-590-02566-X

Everybody Needs a Rock
by Byrd Baylor
Charles Scribner's Sons, New York
ISBN 0-684-13899-9 (cloth)
ISBN 0-684-16011-0 (paper)

I'm Terrific
by Marjorie Weinman Sharmat
Holiday House, New York
ISBN 0-8234-0282-7

Ira Sleeps Over
by Bernard Waber
Houghton Mifflin Company, Boston
ISBN 0-395-13893-0 (cloth)
ISBN 0-395-20503-4 (paper)

Jumanji
by Chris Van Allsburg
Houghton Mifflin Company, Boston
ISBN 0-395-30448-2

Strega Nona
by Tomie de Paola
Prentice-Hall Inc., Englewood Cliffs, N.J.
ISBN 0-13-851600-6 (cloth)
ISBN o-13-851592-1 (paper)

The Tenth Good Thing About Barney
by Judith Viorst
Atheneum
ISBN 0-689-70416-X

That Terrible Halloween Night
by James Stevenson
Greenwillow Books, New York
ISBN 0-688-80281-8

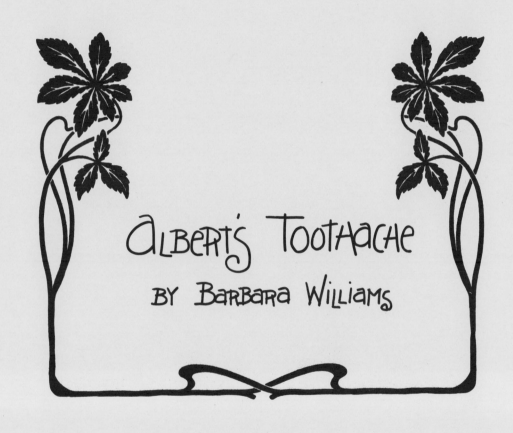

Albert's Toothache

by Barbara Williams

Albert's Toothache
by Barbara Williams

Suggestions for Extended Activities

Discussion:

1. Why wouldn't it be possible for Albert Turtle to
    have a toothache?

2. Think of other animals Barbara Williams might have
    used for her story. For example, an octopus might
    have had a blister on its toe.

3. What do you think about Albert's mother spending
    time worrying in her worrying chair, her worrying
    swing, her worrying rock, and her worrying sofa?

4. Why did Albert's grandmother understand him when
    his mother and father didn't?

5. How do you feel when your parents don't believe
    you?

6. How would the story have ended if Albert's grand-
    mother hadn't come to visit?

Other:

Encourage the students to find some friends to be the
various characters (Albert's mother, Albert's father,
Marybelle, Homer, Albert, and grandmother) and act out
the story as a play.

Study Albert's bedspread. Using a pencil, design a bedspread you would like for your room. Add many details.

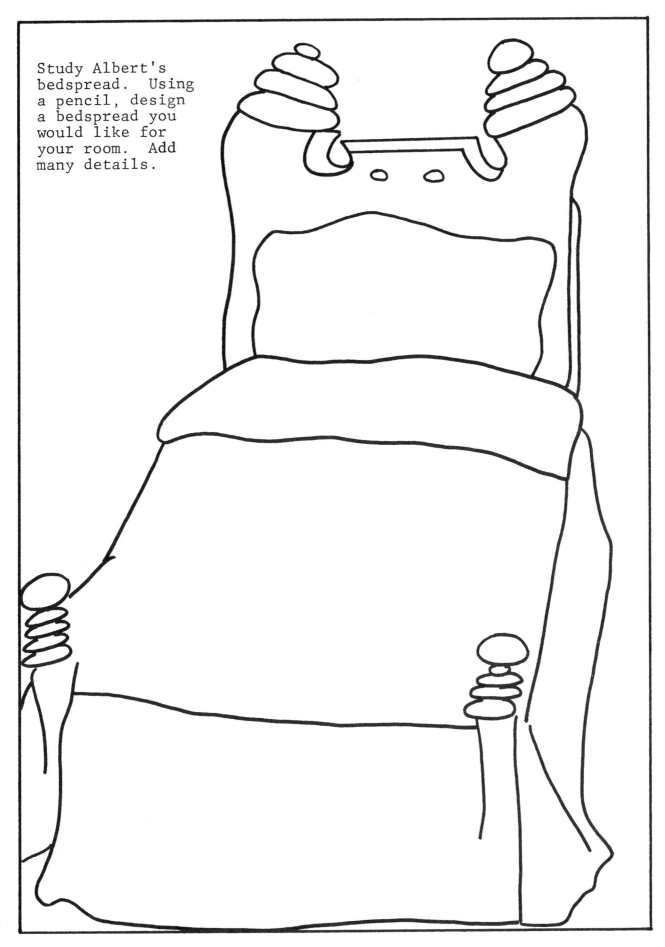

There are well-dressed foolish ideas
just as there are well-dressed fools.

- Nicholas Chamfort

Blissful Breakfasts

Albert's special breakfast consisted of rotting oak bark garnished with sunflower seeds, a dry aspen leaf, and half a green caterpillar. What would you serve for a special breakfast to each of the following:

a monkey _____

_____

_____

a giraffe _____

_____

_____

a whale _____

_____

_____

a robin _____

_____

_____

a horse _____

_____

_____

YOU! _____

_____

I am a great believer in luck, and I find the
harder I work the more I have of it.

- Stephen Leacock

TURTLE TERMINOLOGY

Name / **Research** / **Albert's Toothache**

What do these turtle terms refer to?

carapace _____

plastron _____

scutes _____

terrapin _____

tortoise _____

Describe the physical characteristic each of these turtles is known for:

Painted _____

Western Pond _____

Spotted _____

Wood _____

Softshell _____

Leatherback _____

Draw lines to match the following:

Ugliest   Leatherback

Smallest   Green

Largest   Musk

Best to Eat   Alligator Snapping

Most Beautiful   Bog

Smelliest   Hawksbill

Answer True (T) or False (F):

___ All turtles are hatched from eggs.
___ Turtles are deaf.
___ Turtles are the only reptiles that have shells.
___ Turtles are color-blind.
___ Turtles have little or no voice.
___ All turtles have webbed feet.
___ Turtles have teeth.

In which part of the world would you find these turtles? (Be specific.)

Diamondback Terrapin _____

Alligator Snapping _____

Tornier's Tortoise _____

Side-necked _____

Sawback _____

Map Turtle _____

Hawksbill _____

There are over 200 different species of turtles alive today. Can you list many of the 38 found in North America?

TURTLE TERMINOLOGY

KEY

Name · *Research* · *Albert's Toothache*

What do these turtle terms refer to?

carapace __UPPER SHELL__

plastron __LOWER SHELL__

scutes __HORNY SCALES__

terrapin __FRESH WATER TURTLE__

tortoise __LAND TURTLE__

Describe the physical characteristic each of these turtles is known for:

Painted __RED MARKINGS__

Western Pond __BLACK__

Spotted __YELLOW__

Wood __ORANGE__

Softshell __LOOKS LIKE A PANCAKE__

Leatherback __LEATHERY SKIN__

Draw lines to match the following:

Ugliest — Alligator Snapping

Smallest — Bog

Largest — Leatherback

Best to Eat — Green

Most Beautiful — Hawksbill

Smelliest — Musk

Answer True (T) or False (F):

__T__ All turtles are hatched from eggs.

__T__ Turtles are deaf.

__T__ Turtles are the only reptiles that have shells.

__F__ Turtles are color-blind.

__T__ Turtles have little or no voice.

__F__ All turtles have webbed feet.

__F__ Turtles have teeth.

In which part of the world would you find these turtles? (Be specific.)

Diamondback Terrapin __GULF OF MEXICO & ATLANTIC COAST__

Alligator Snapping __CENTRAL & SOUTH-EASTERN U.S.__

Tornier's Tortoise __AFRICA__

Side-necked __SOUTH AMERICA, AFRICA__

Spotted __EAST COAST, U.S.__

Map Turtle __SOUTHERN CANADA, MIDWEST U.S.__

Hawksbill __CARIBBEAN__

There are over 200 different species of turtles alive today. Can you list many of the 38 found in North America?

BREAD and JAM
FOR FRANCES

BY

RUSSELL HOBAN

Bread and Jam for Frances
by Russell Hoban

Suggestions for Extended Activities

Discussion:

1. One reason Francis didn't like to try new foods was
   because she always knew what she was getting when
   she ate bread and jam. What are other reasons people
   don't try new foods?

2. In what order do you like to eat your food? Albert
   liked having his come out even. Some people like to
   eat things they dislike first. Encourage students
   to explain their responses.

3. What do you think of the way Frances' mother solved
   the problem?

4. Frances' mother and father developed a plan to have
   her tire of bread and jam so she would eat other foods.
   Discuss other situations (e.g. cleaning your bedroom,
   doing homework) and design plans that parents might
   use to help their children.

Other:

1. This book may be useful in a unit on nutrition.

2. Read aloud chapter 1 of How to Eat Like a Child
   by Delia Ephron.

FOOD, GLORIOUS FOOD

You've won a week of sack lunches from a famous restaurant! Consult Albert's and Frances' lunches for ideas to help you plan each day's menu.

Name	MONDAY	TUESDAY	WEDNESDAY
Originality	THURSDAY	FRIDAY	
Bread and Jam For Frances			

A man without mirth is like a wagon without springs: he is jolted disagreeably by every pebble in the road.

- Henry Ward Beecher

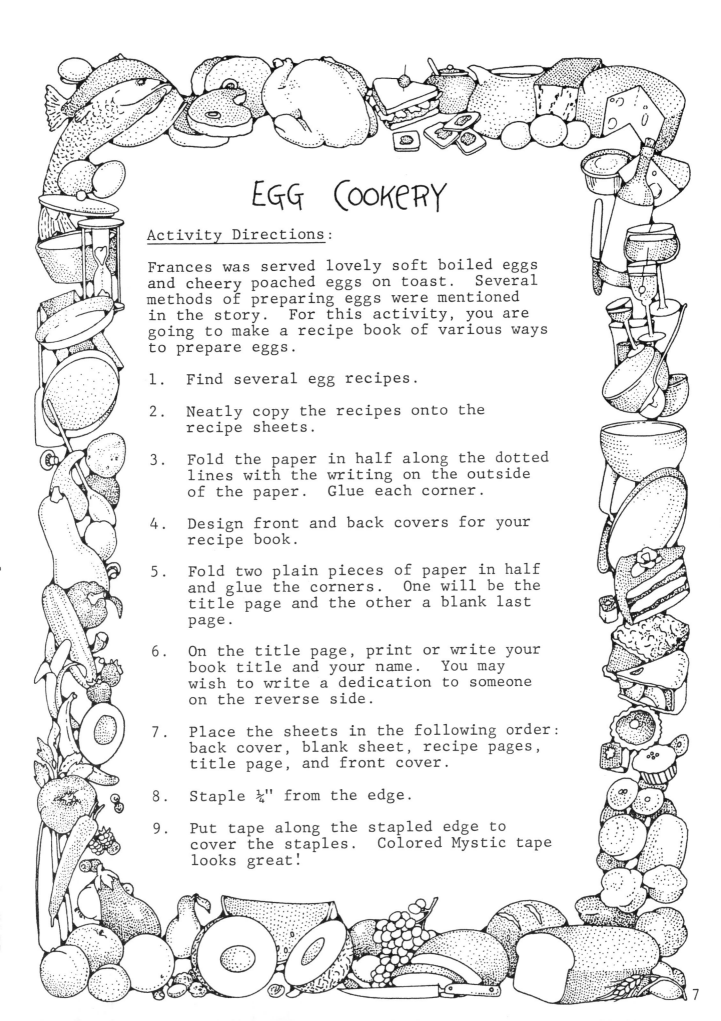

EGG COOKERY

Activity Directions:

Frances was served lovely soft boiled eggs and cheery poached eggs on toast. Several methods of preparing eggs were mentioned in the story. For this activity, you are going to make a recipe book of various ways to prepare eggs.

1. Find several egg recipes.

2. Neatly copy the recipes onto the recipe sheets.

3. Fold the paper in half along the dotted lines with the writing on the outside of the paper. Glue each corner.

4. Design front and back covers for your recipe book.

5. Fold two plain pieces of paper in half and glue the corners. One will be the title page and the other a blank last page.

6. On the title page, print or write your book title and your name. You may wish to write a dedication to someone on the reverse side.

7. Place the sheets in the following order: back cover, blank sheet, recipe pages, title page, and front cover.

8. Staple ¼" from the edge.

9. Put tape along the stapled edge to cover the staples. Colored Mystic tape looks great!

Recipe:
From:
Serves:

Recipe:
From:
Serves:

I love eggplant ?

Read the song that Frances wrote telling how she felt about eggs.

Choose 2 foods you dislike and write a song for each. (Hint: it's easier to write if you keep a popular tune in mind.)

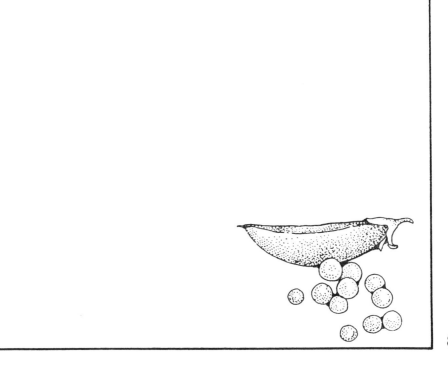

Name

Originality

Bread and Jam For Francis

Quality is never an accident; it is always the result of intelligent effort.

- John Ruskin

WHAT are YOU eating

AND WHERE DID IT COME FROM?

North America is a 'melting pot' of food as well as people. Use
cookbooks and dictionaries to find out about these foods.

	WHAT is it?	WHERE DID it come from?
1. Vichyssoise		
2. Sweetbreads		
3. Tabouli		
4. Petit fours		
5. Succotash		
6. Cafe au lait		
7. Coq au vin		
8. Mincemeat		
9. Ambrosia		
10. Welsh rarebit		
11. Waldorf salad		
12. Weiner schnitzel		
13. Eggs Benedict		
14. Black Forest cake		
15. Gazpacho		

Name

Research

Bread and Jam For Francis

WHaT aRe YOU eaTING

AND WHERE DID IT COME FROM?

North America is a 'melting pot' of food as well as people. Use cookbooks and dictionaries to find out about these foods.

	WHaT is it?	WHeRe DID it Come FROM?
1. Vichyssoise	a COLD SOUP, MaDe OF LeeKS, POTaTOeS, CReaM & CHICKeN STOCK	FRaNCe
2. Sweetbreads	THe THYMUS GLaND OF a CaLF, USUaLLY CReaMeD, BROILeD OR BReaDeD	ENGLaND
3. Tabouli	a SaLaD MaDe OF BULGHUR WHeaT, PaRSLeY, TOMaTOeS aND CUCUMBeR	LeBaNON
4. Petit fours	SMaLL Tea CaKeS, FROSTeD & OFTeN DeCORaTeD WITH FLOWeRS	FRaNCe
5. Succotash	LIMa BeaNS & GReeN CORN, COOKeD TOGeTHeR	aLGONQUIaN INDIaNS
6. Cafe au lait	COFFee WITH HOT MILK, IN aBOUT eQUaL PaRTS	FRaNCe
7. Coq au vin	CHICKeN IN ReD WINe SaUCe	FRaNCe
8. Mincemeat	a FINeLY CHOPPeD MIXTURe OF RaISINS, aPPLeS, SPICeS, WITH OR WITHOUT MeaT	ENGLaND
9. Ambrosia	a DeSSeRT MaDe OF ORaNGeS & SHReDDeD COCONUT	GReeCe
10. Welsh rarebit	MeLTeD CHeeSe, MIXeD WITH MILK OR BeeR, SeRVeD OVeR TOaST	WaLeS / ENGLaND
11. Waldorf salad	a SaLaD MaDe OF DICeD aPPLeS, CeLeRY, NUTS & MaYONNaISe	New YORK
12. Weiner schnitzel	THIN, BReaDeD VeaL CUTLeT	GeRMaNY
13. Eggs Benedict	POaCHeD eGGS & BROILeD HaM ON TOaSTeD HaLVeS OF ENGLISH MUFFIN COVeReD WITH SaUCe	U.S.
14. Black Forest cake	a CHOCOLaTe CaKe, WITH CHeRRY FILLING	GeRMaNY
15. Gazpacho	a COLD SOUP MaDe OF RaW, CHOPPeD VeGeTaBLeS	SPaIN

Name

Research

Bread and Jam For Francis

EVERYBODY
NEEDS a ROCK

BY   BYRD   BAYLOR

Everybody Needs a Rock
by Byrd Baylor

Suggestions for Extended Activities

Art:

Choose a smooth rock and use acrylics to decorate and
paint a message on it.

Other:

1. Have the students look carefully at the style of writing
    with the unusual use of lines. They may want to
    experiment writing a poem or a few sentences about
    themselves imitating that style.

2. Information: This book was an American Library
    Association Notable Book.

Name ——————

Fluency

Everybody Needs a Rock

1. ———————————	21. ———————————
2. ———————————	22. ———————————
3. ———————————	23. ———————————
4. ———————————	24. ———————————
5. ———————————	25. ———————————
6. ———————————	26. ———————————
7. ———————————	27. ———————————
8. ———————————	28. ———————————
9. ———————————	29. ———————————
10. ———————————	30. ———————————
11. ———————————	31. ———————————
12. ———————————	32. ———————————
13. ———————————	33. ———————————
14. ———————————	34. ———————————
15. ———————————	35. ———————————
16. ———————————	36. ———————————
17. ———————————	37. ———————————
18. ———————————	38. ———————————
19. ———————————	39. ———————————
20. ———————————	40. ———————————

THINK...

of many possible ways
you could use a ROCK.

A list of 25 is good,
30 is super, 35 is
excellent and 40 or
more is fantastic!

11

Children are remarkable for their intelligence and ardor, for their curiosity, their intolerance of shams, the clarity and ruthlessness of their vision.

— Aldous Huxley

The author, Byrd Baylor, has stated that everybody needs a rock. What else does everybody need? A plant? A marble? A pet? Choose something you think everybody needs and list ten different reasons why everybody needs this item.

EveryBody Needs a _____

Far away in the sunshine are my highest inspira-
tions. I may not reach them, but I can look up
and see the beauty, believe in them and try to
follow where they lead.

- Louisa May Alcott

Think of a game that uses one person and a rock. List the rules and write a paragraph to explain the object of the game.

_____

_____

_____

_____

_____

_____

_____

_____

_____

_____

_____

_____

_____

The best effect of any book is that it excites the reader to self-activity.

- Thomas Carlyle

INSPIRED ILLUSTRATIONS

The book's illustrations are very unusual. Study
them carefully. Write what you like about them
and what you dislike about them. Try to keep both
columns equal. Circle your strongest like and your
strongest dislike.

Likes	Dislikes

Gnawing on bones of contention provides little nourishment.

- Arnold Glasow

Everybody Needs A Rock

Research   Name ———————

There are 3 kinds of rocks: igneous, sedimentary and
metamorphic. Place each of these rocks in the
appropriate category.

granite   shales   fossils
slate   phyllite   pumice
pegmatite   hornfels   obsidian
sandstone   marble   conglomerates
peridotite   quartzite   limestone

IGNEOUS Rocks are formed at high temperatures.	SEDIMENTARY Rocks are formed by action of water, wind or organic agents.	METAMORPHIC Rocks have been changed by heat, pressure or chemical action.

Everybody Needs A Rock

Research

Name _____ KEY

There are 3 kinds of rocks: igneous, sedimentary and metamorphic. Place each of these rocks in the appropriate category.

granite   shales   fossils
slate   phyllite   pumice
pegmatite   hornfels   obsidian
sandstone   marble   conglomerates
peridotite   quartzite   limestone

IGNEOUS Rocks are formed at high temperatures.	SEDIMENTARY Rocks are formed by action of water, wind or organic agents.	METAMORPHIC Rocks have been changed by heat, pressure or chemical action.
GRANITE PEGMATITE PUMICE OBSIDIAN PERIDOTITE	SANDSTONE SHALES LIMESTONE CONGLOMERATES FOSSILS	SLATE MARBLE QUARTZITE PHYLLITE

I'M TERRIFIC

BY Marjorie Weinman Sharmat

I'm Terrific
by Marjorie Weinman Sharmat

Suggestions for Extended Activities

Discussion:

1. Compare the reactions of Mrs. Bear in I'm Terrific and the reactions of the mother in Albert's Toothache.

2. If Jason had never changed, what would his life have been like?

3. Why isn't it socially acceptable to compliment yourself?

4. Is there such a thing as too much self esteem? Can a person be too good (for their own good)?

5. Think about something in yourself you'd like to change. How would you go about doing it?

6. People frequently try out new ways to act, speak, write and look. Encourage students to share a change they tried to make, and the results.

7. You are terrific because you are unique. What is there about you that makes you unique?

8. Share New Year's Resolutions you've tried.

TRULY TERRIFIC !!

What <u>different</u> <u>kinds</u> of
terrific things do you do?

Idea	Category
WASH DISHES	HELP MOTHER

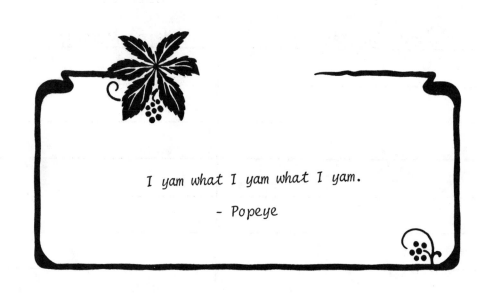

I yam what I yam what I yam.

- Popeye

I'm Terrific   Description Within Categories   Name

Think of your terrific behavior. List terrific things you do that are:

THREE STAR

TWO STAR

ONE STAR

People have one thing in common: they are all different.

- Robert Zend

I'M TERRIFIC !

List adjectives about yourself that begin with each letter.

The man who limits his interests
limits his life.

- Vincent Price

Plan a terrific activity to do for someone you think
is terrific. You might wish to make something for
them (e.g. a card) or do something for them.

WHAT I'm going to do:

_____

MATERIALS I'll need:

_____

_____

_____

STEPS I'll take: (in order)

1. _____

2. _____

3. _____

4. _____

5. _____

6. _____

7. _____

8. _____

9. _____

10. _____

PROBLEMS I may have:

_____   _____

_____   _____

_____   _____

Name

Planning

I'm Terrific

A man wrapped up in himself makes a very small bundle.

- Benjamin Franklin

Ira Sleeps Over

by Bernard Waber

Ira Sleeps Over
by Bernard Waber

Suggestions for Extended Activities

Discussion:

Ira was afraid Reggie would laugh if he brought his
teddy bear. Why? Can you think of a time you were afraid
someone would laugh at you?

Art:

Draw a picture of the best time you ever had playing with
a friend.

Creative Writing:

1. How would the ending be different if Reggie did not
    get out his teddy bear?

2. Ira's sister was a pest! Write about a time when
    your brother/sister was a pest to you.

Other:

Act this book out as a radio play. The characters are:
Ira, Ira's sister, Ira's mother, Ira's father, Reggie and
Reggie's father.

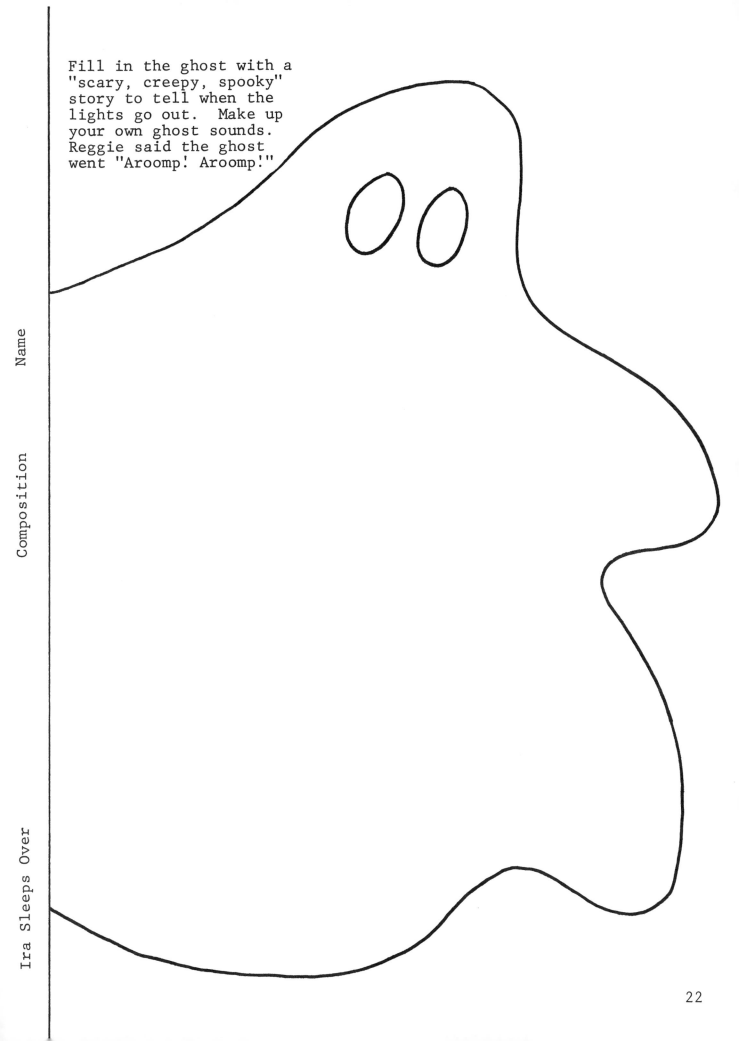

Fill in the ghost with a
"scary, creepy, spooky"
story to tell when the
lights go out. Make up
your own ghost sounds.
Reggie said the ghost
went "Aroomp! Aroomp!"

Name

Composition

Ira Sleeps Over

You can't have a better tomorrow if
you are thinking about yesterday
all the time.

- Charles F. Kettering

SCRUPULOUSLY SCIENTIFIC SURVEY

Survey at least 20 classmates to find out what their favorite stuffed animal was when they were young. Their choices are: a dog, cat, teddy bear, other choice, or liked none.

SURVEY (use tally marks ⧄⧄⧄)

dog _____

cat _____

teddy bear _____

other choice _____

none _____

Now make a bar graph, circle graph, or picture graph to show your findings. Be sure to include a title and a key.

All glory comes from daring to begin.

- Eugene F. Ware

Teddy Bears

What would you like to know about teddy bears? Think of 4 to 6 questions you have and then find the answers. Share your findings with a friend (and your teddy bear).

Question 1: _____

    Answer: _____

    Resource: _____

Question 2: _____

    Answer: _____

    Resource: _____

Question 3: _____

    Answer: _____

    Resource: _____

Question 4: _____

    Answer: _____

    Resource: _____

Question 5: _____

    Answer: _____

    Resource: _____

Question 6: _____

    Answer: _____

    Resource: _____

What fire could ever equal the
sunshine of a winter's day?

- Henry David Thoreau

Tah Tah?   Foo Foo?

Survey your classmates to find out the names of stuffed animals they have had.

Student's Name	Stuffed Animal's Name

Name

Research

Ira Sleeps Over

25

Time flies, but, remember you're the navigator.

Jumanji

BY Chris Van Allsburg

Jumanji
by Chris Van Allsburg

Suggestions for Extended Activities

Discussion:

1. The jungle came to Peter and Judy. How would the
story have been different if they had been transported
to the jungle?

2. Describe what might have happened if the game had been
Monopoly or Clue?

3. Discuss unusual rules students have encountered in
games they have played.

Creative Writing:

Write a follow-up story in which Danny and Walter Budwing
play Jumanji.

Other:

Plan an afternoon in which students bring games to play and
share.

a BookMark Marks the Spot

Study the drawings in <u>Jumanji</u> and use a pencil to design a
bookmark in the same style. Pay attention to shading your
drawings. Have the title <u>Jumanji</u> somewhere on the bookmark.
Ideas for decoration are: a lion, a python, board game,
rhinoceros, raindrops, volcano, guide, monkeys... You may
wish to use clear contact paper on both sides to make your
bookmark more durable.

Name

Elaboration

Jumanji

Time is but the stream I go a-fishing in.

- Henry David Thoreau

You've been given this format to create a game. Decide on an
attractive name and theme and establish appropriate rules.
You may want to include an unusual rule like Jumanji had.

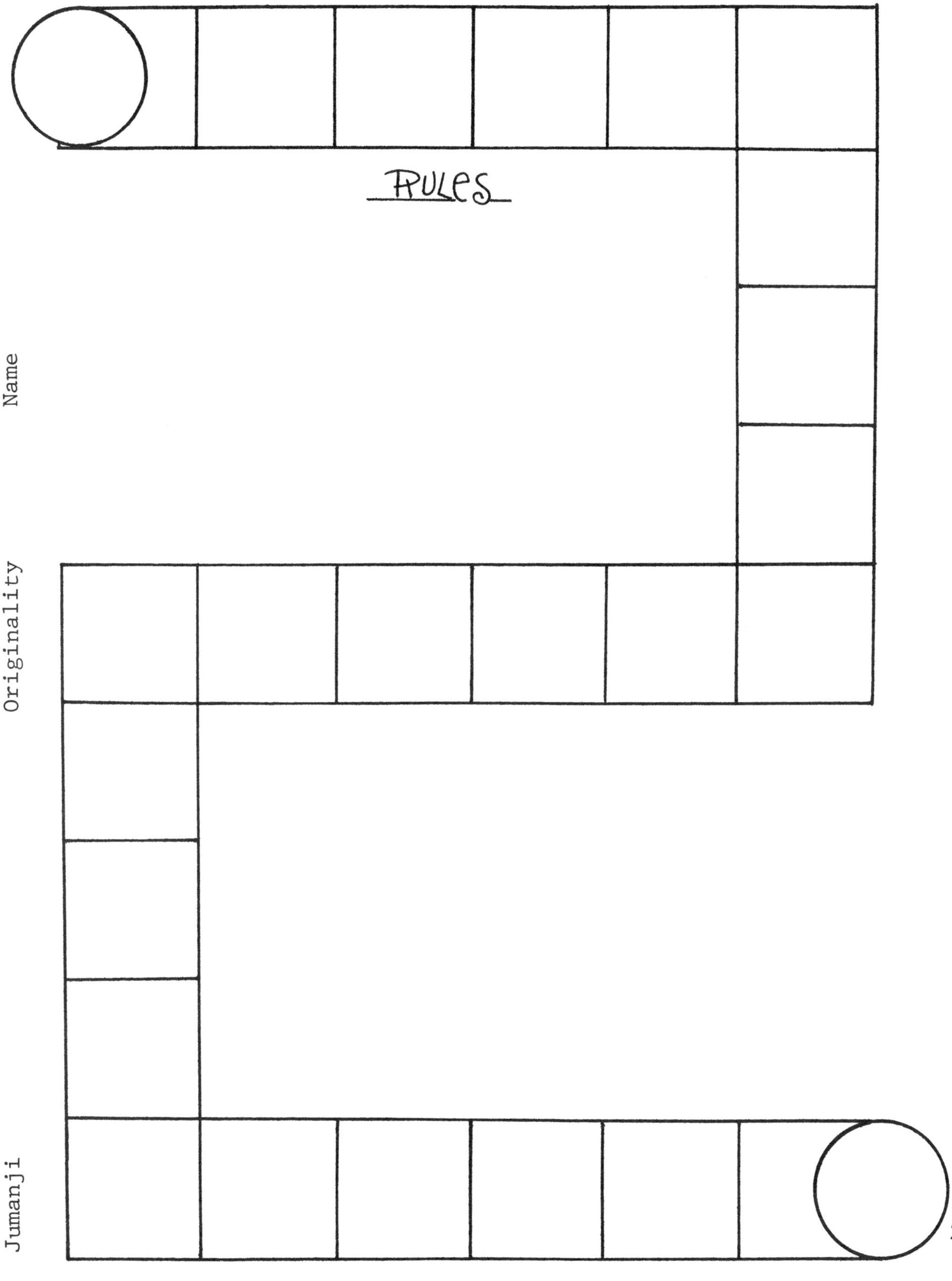

RULES

Name

Originality

Jumanji

28

The trees were full of silver-white
sunlight and the meanest of them
sparkled.

- Flannery O'Connor

FORECASTING

Mother and Dad arrived home from the opera early.
List many possible causes why this happened. List
many effects of their unexpected return.

Causes	Effects

Mother tells me "Happy dreams!" and takes away the light,
An' leaves me lyin' all alone an' seein' things at night.

- Eugene Field

Nuts about Games

Think of a game that begins with each letter of the alphabet!

Name

A _____   B _____

          C _____

D _____   E _____

          F _____

G _____   H _____

          I _____

J _____   K _____

          L _____

M _____   N _____

          O _____

P _____   Q _____

          R _____

S _____   T _____

          U _____

V _____   W _____

          X _____

Y _____   Z _____

Jumanji

Imagination is more important than knowledge.

- Albert Einstein

Strega Nona

by Tomie de Paola

Strega Nona
by Tomie De Paola

Suggestions for Extended Activities

Discussion:

1. Where do you think the town of Calabria is located? Use story clues to explain your answer.

2. What four items do you think Strega Nona put in the potion to get rid of warts?

3. In several illustrations you will notice a rabbit. Why do you think Tomie De Paola drew the rabbit on the roof?

4. Discuss the many animals and the frequency of their appearance in the illustrations. What is their significance to the story?

5. In what ways do you think the town could have protected itself from the pasta?

6. Strega Nona said that the punishment must fit the crime. What does this mean? How could we do this in our classroom? How is this done or not done in our society?

MAGiC CHef

Think of your favorite food. Write a four
line verse to instruct the magic pot to
make this food, a four line verse to stop,
and a gesture you would use instead of
three kisses.

I want the magic pot to make:

_____

My verse to begin:

_____

_____

_____

_____

My verse to end:

_____

_____

_____

_____

My gesture:

_____

When you play, play with all your might,
but when you work, don't play at all.

- Theodore Roosevelt

DESIGNER HATS

dePaola displays an amazing variety of headcoverings in <u>Strega Nona</u>. Create 3 of your own, striving for unusual design in each.

Name

Originality

Strega Nona

Learning is like rowing upstream; not to advance is to drop back.

- Chinese saying

HELPING OCCUPATIONS

People went to see Strega Nona because she helped them. Be fluent and list at least 50 occupations that help people.

Name

Fluency

Strega Nona

The world is a beautiful book, but of little
use to him who cannot read it.

- Goldoni

The Tenth Good Thing
About Barney

BY   Judith Viorst

The Tenth Good Thing About Barney
by Judith Viorst

Suggestions for Extended Activities

Discussion:

1. Why do we have funerals for pets that have died?

2. You had a dream that you were at the funeral for Barney because you were the boy's best friend. What did you say to comfort him?

Creative Writing:

Write a speech to give at your pet's funeral.

Other:

1. Find out if there is a pet cemetary in your area. What costs are involved in burying a pet there?

2. Reading this book may be a way to begin a unit or study on death and dying.

Name That Animal !

Barney was an unusual name for a cat.
Think of unusual names for a ...

goldfish _____

hamster _____

guinea pig _____

toad _____

salamander _____

chicken _____

horse _____

monkey _____

dog _____

canary _____

mouse _____

turtle _____

parrot _____

butterfly _____

pig (besides Charlotte) _____

spider _____

rabbit _____

squirrel _____

cactus plant _____

36

It is not only fine feathers that
make fine birds.

- Aesop

The Tenth Good Thing About Barney   Composition   Name ———————

I LIKE YOU! Select a person you care about. Neatly write or print the title, "The Ten Good Things About ". List ten good things about that person and give it to them.

What you do speaks so loud that I cannot hear what you say.

- Ralph Waldo Emerson

Pet Practicalities

Should you have a pet? List the advantages and disadvantages of having a pet, making sure you have an equal number of points for each side. In conclusion, circle the strongest advantage and the strongest disadvantage.

Advantages	Disadvantages

Name

Evaluation

The Tenth Good Thing About Barney

I escaped into fantasy when I was young and grew up with fiction. Four of the most meaningful words I know are: 'Once upon a time.'

- Robert Redford

That Terrible
Halloween Night

By James Stevenson

That Terrible Halloween Night
by James Stevenson

Suggestions for Extended Activities

Discussion:

1. What happened to Gramdpa behind the purple striped door?

2. Discuss things that frequently appear in books and movies as scary. Why do they make us afraid?

3. Do you and your grandparents think the same things are funny?

Other:

1. Find out about the origin of Halloween.

2. Ask your grandparents about a time when they were frightened.

WHAT SHOULD I WEAR?

It's Halloween and you need a costume. List many Halloween costumes. Circle the costume you think you would like the best.

If you have built castles in the air, your
work need not be lost. Now put foundations
under them.

- Osa Johnson

Worst Parts

Draw a picture of an imaginary creature that is the worst parts of lots of things. Use details!

I wanted to live deep and suck out
all the marrow of life.

- Henry David Thoreau

Think about Halloween night. What do you like?
What do you dislike? Keep both columns even!
Circle your strongest like and your strongest
dislike.

Halloween

Likes | Dislikes

I never saw a moor;
I never saw the sea;
Yet know I how the heather looks
And what a wave must be.

- Emily Dickinson

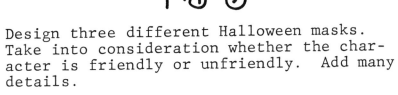

MASKS

Design three different Halloween masks.
Take into consideration whether the char-
acter is friendly or unfriendly. Add many
details.

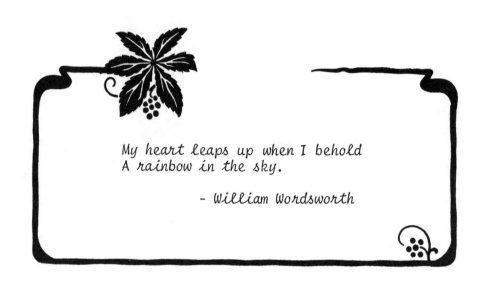

My heart leaps up when I behold
A rainbow in the sky.

- William Wordsworth

THERE WILL BE NO OBSERVANCE OF HALLOWEEN

Think of many reasons why
this law was passed. What
will happen as a result?

CAUSES	EFFECTS

It is better to ask some questions than
to know all the answers.

- James Thurber

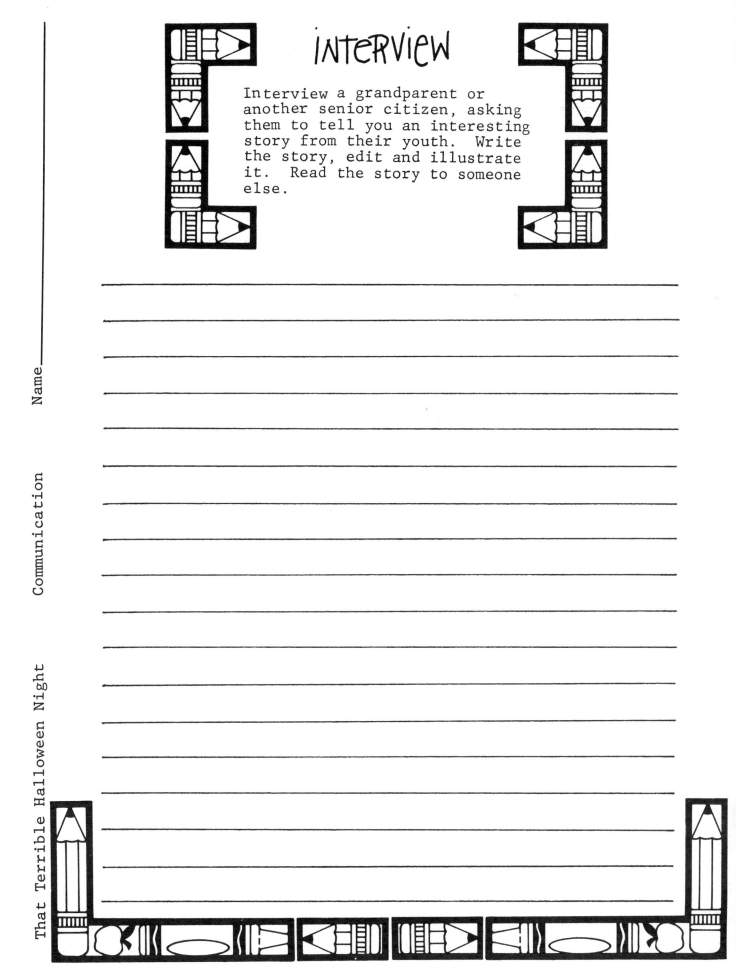

INTERVIEW

Interview a grandparent or another senior citizen, asking them to tell you an interesting story from their youth. Write the story, edit and illustrate it. Read the story to someone else.

Name

Communication

That Terrible Halloween Night

Four things come not back:
The spoken word;
The sped arrow;
Time past;
The neglected opportunity.

- Omar Iba

Research   Name

Aall of Fame

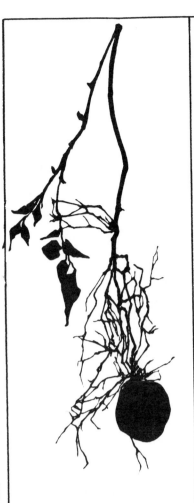

All of these Americans continued to have outstanding careers as senior citizens. Describe significant accomplishments of each, <u>after</u> the age of 65.

SUSAN B. ANTHONY 1820 – 1906	PETER COOPER 1791–1883
	BENJAMIN FRANKLIN 1706 – 1790
MARTHA GRAHAM 1894 –	RONALD REAGAN 1911 –
	GRANDMA MOSES 1860 – 1961
DOUGLAS MacARTHUR 1880 – 1964	OLIVER WENDELL HOLMES, JR. 1841 – 1935
	LAURA INGALLS WILDER 1867 – 1957

Hall of Fame

All of these Americans continued to have outstanding careers as senior citizens. Describe significant accomplishments of each, after the age of 65.

BENJAMIN FRANKLIN 1706 - 1790

- American Commissioner and Minister to France at age 70

- Became President of the Executive Council of Pennsylvania

PETER COOPER 1791-1883

- Founded Cooper Union for the Advancement of Science and Art at age 66

- Ran for U.S. President at age 85.

SUSAN B. ANTHONY 1820 - 1906

- An international leader in the woman suffrage cause. She continued to speak for this cause into her mid-80s.

GRANDMA MOSES 1860 - 1961

- Took up painting at age 67 and became famous for her primitive folk art style. She continued to paint and hold exhibits until after the age of 100.

RONALD REAGAN 1911 -

- Became President of the United States at age 70.

MARTHA GRAHAM 1894 -

- A dancer and choreographer, she continued to dance until age 75.

- At age 79, she published her Notebooks, a basic source for choreography

---

LAURA INGALLS WILDER 1867 - 1957

- At age 65, began writing the "Little House" books

OLIVER WENDELL HOLMES, JR. 1841 - 1935

- A lawyer, Holmes served on the U.S. Supreme Court until his retirement at age 90.

DOUGLAS MacARTHUR 1880 - 1964

- Was made Commander of the United Nations forces fighting in Korea